GREEN VISTAS

GREEN VISTAS

by Charles Pierre

Halyard Press
New York

ISBN 978-0-615-30669-8

This is a revised edition of **Green Vistas**, first published by Northpoint Press in 1981.

Acknowledgments

I wish to thank the editors of the following literary journals, in which some of these poems first appeared:

The Aurorean; Avocet; Bellowing Ark; BigCityLit.com; Hidden Oak; Manhattan Linear; Parnassus Literary Journal; Soul Fountain; Voices International; Waterways.

"The Swan" contains a phrase from John Keats's "Sleep and Poetry"; "Solar Eclipse" includes a phrase from Samuel Taylor Coleridge's "Love's Apparition and Evanishment"; and "The Bond" uses four phrases from Psalm 90 (The New English Bible).

Also by Charles Pierre

Father of Water (Black Buzzard Press, 2008)

Cover Painting: *Green Vistas* **by Sica**

 Produced at The Print Center, Inc. 225 Varick St., New York, NY 10014, a non-profit facility for literary and arts-related publications. (212) 206-8465

Contents

Self-Portrait

Since dusk, I have been sitting peacefully
among the objects of my room: table
and chair, a small notepad, and in my hand,
a silver pen. There's a sense of wholeness
within me now, and it seems to extend
throughout this space. The light and shadow
on my walls and floor are nothing apart
from all that is visible. A tall lamp
in the corner has been useful to me
at times when books were my only release,
but tonight my eyes, shaded by dark lines
of sleeplessness, are resting in a glow,
whose origin is nowhere to be seen.

The Pendant of Childhood

A silver fish on a silver chain
once swam in the air beneath my shirt.
I would follow him down to the channels
of his world, hidden from the hard light of day,

out through the gates of the Mill Pond,
around the dock at Centerport
and the sandbars of Fleet's Cove,
along Asharoken beach and past Eaton's Neck,

where the water was green, clear and open,
and nothing ever slowed our voyage,
and almost all that we ever did
was left to the timeless sea.

Helena

She returns to the shore in dream each night
to walk the wet sands of Pori, her home
on the coast of Finland, where waves rise
and break around her body, fine spray
from the combers seeping into her hair
and lashes and coating her skin with salt,
as she passes along miles of empty beach
through the brief darkness of summer,
the night, land and sea united as one
in her sleeping eyes, until the loose grains
underfoot disperse, and the far waters
of Northern Europe dry up, when she wakes
to the rushing dawn of her New York life.

The Swan

A plume of smoke from my campfire
takes the shape of a pale swan

that glides over a Montauk lake
above the light-flecked ripples,

the body with a long curved neck
and rounded chest climbing the air

through thin filaments of sun
in the humid haze of summer,

while it passes across the crest
of a dune near the water's edge,

quickening in pace when a gust
nudges the weightless wings and feet,

only to slow at tufts of sedge
beside a path to the ocean,

the *trains of peaceful images*
dimming as afternoon wanes,

and the solitary bird
dissolves in an evening breeze.

The Resemblance

In the way she held the flower,
each became more of the other
as the sameness in their shapes
and the interplay between them
emerged before our steady gaze.

Here were folds within folds,
she with long slender arms
folded upon each other, and
the long-stemmed flower, folded
into itself, held in her arms,

the aura of each a part of the other,
the frail lines of each balancing
the other, and the color of each
reflected in the other's glow—
a blond-haired girl, a yellow rose.

Twilight Wine

Swirling in my glass are the hues
of an evening sky, dusky red
and deep blue, where reflected stars
glitter across the dark liquid.

When I lift these sunset colors
to my lips, a shimmering stream
spills over the rim, as mingled
wine and starlight flow into me.

Big Fresh Pond

A gusty wind ruffles the edges of lily pads
and turns up the light undersides of leaves
on oaks and maples surrounding this pond
amid the Southampton woods of late July,
while two girls in a sailboat tack back and
forth from shore to shore with casual skill,
one seated at the stern, her slim hands
gripping the tiller and mainsheet, the other
kneeling amidships, raising or lowering
the daggerboard as the depth requires,
their sharp voices carrying the full length
of sun-plated water, the two thin figures
shifting from side to side within the boat
each time they come about, heads down
when the boom swings over them,
the sail going slack for a long moment,
then catching a breeze and puffing out
with a muffled snap as their trim craft
makes crossing after crossing, until
they spot dark clouds above and veer
toward a shaded cove, where the girls
anchor in the shallows and wade ashore,
just before the wind and sunlight fade,
and the first few drops of rain hit
the lily pads and leaves with quiet *ticks*.

Riverside Park

In the airless shade of dazed honey locusts,
I trudge an asphalt ledge above the ashen Hudson,
where August haze spreads across this wet desert,
and yellow sludge laps the crusted bank below,
where bursts of high sun torch this rusted railing
and every cursed thing under the scorch of noon.

September Sky

Countless stars in the spangled fury hold my eyes
in their glow, as I sit alone on a Northport beach
at midnight, the dark tide rolling with elastic shine;
the bits of kelp, quartz, shell, and bone sparkling
at my feet. I see starlight on the sails of a sloop
tacking across the harbor, on the hulls and masts
of yachts huddled at a marina, and on the roofs
of houses in the surrounding hills. And I wonder
at the power of this bold light to merge with all
before me, even coating the strokes of wet ink
from my pen as I write these words in my pad;
and wonder, too, that the stars burning above
might have died eons ago, their glow an illusion,
and the lines of intense light just long frayed ends.

Hands

The gestures she made with her hands when speaking
seemed to span the currents of misunderstanding
between us, though her words said nothing of me.

I saw the hands fall, as if from a failure of love,
to separate sides of her body, then spring up
together, in a prayer-like clasp at heart level.

And while she spoke, brushing the front of my shirt
with a finger, it seemed we were sailing in the same
direction, though her words said nothing of me.

October

Each tree withholds the flow
of sap from branch to leaf,
and the specter of death
spreads across the woodlands,
where seasonal flowers pale
before the blaze of foliage.

I watch the long cortege
of red, orange, yellow,
gold, brown and purple
pass in the cool air,
without any sorrow
at this funeral of the year.

Forgetful of all the lost
greenery, my sharp need
for color fed once again,
I hike a scenic trail at dusk
with dry autumn eyes
to catch the last bright flash.

Lang's Pond

When afternoon is almost gone
and the season lost in the hour,

this quiet place envelopes all
in the soft aura of water

that is flecked and streaked
with slowly changing light,

where geese meander and
preen at the shoreline,

and squirrels high in the oaks
mend their nests with leaves,

and doves, their deep-throated
notes lingering in the air,

peck at bits of food left
by midday picnickers,

as breezes start to tease up
ripples on the pond's rim,

and glimmers of late sun
dip through distant pines.

Late Autumn at Centerport

Spring unfurled from ripening buds,
and a balmy summer preserved
the deep greens of oak and maple
on hillsides across the harbor.

A month ago, the reds and golds
were bright distractions, but today,
descending a hill to this beach
through the bitter December air,

I feel the withering absence
of colors that once filled the trees.
Fallen leaves are now visible,
black and rotting in the shallows.

Here, the full cycle of seasons
has yet to pass, but today,
having seen this much of the year,
I know my fate ahead of time.

Solar Eclipse

At times
on her flight
through solar space,

the moon,
no longer *pale*
and cold and dim,

glides in front
of the larger earth
to steal the sun's fire,

the black
disk of her face
lit by curls of flame,

as he spins
in the shadow
of her radiance,

his blue sheen
gone ashen gray
in the midday dusk.

Island Corridor

The first sparks of dawn ignite
the skylight of our loft,
each frosted pane of glass
aflame with December sun,
as frigid wind streams in
from the near Atlantic
to riffle the bay and quicken
the early pace of Manhattan
on streets already awake
and prepared for our arrival.

Jolted out of restless sleep
by rapid shouts that mount
from huddles of eager men
in the hectic square below,
we rise to bursts of talk
about business and cash,
the air charged with bids
on cut-rate wares, haggles
for price, and shrill spats
over deals gone bad.

We quit our spacious aerie
for the twists of narrow lanes,
a thirst for sights and sounds
our ticket north past the brash
arenas of downtown finance,
through patches of ethnic color,
cluttered with fabric, watches,
trinkets, handbags and kitsch
hawked at makeshift stands,
our morning walk a zigzag

up the island's hurried byways,
where tense traffic bolts ahead
on revving engines, where men
and women reflected in windows
jump in and out of focus when
truck or bus drums the potholes,
where at every corner, honks
and blares jazz winter's ruckus,
our breath freezing as we go,
the white puffs leading us onward.

The sun continues its steep climb
to our right and advances the day
toward noon. We track its beam
across gritty factory districts,
their docks stacked with freight,
beside paint-spattered studios
burgeoning with art, and beyond
to the brassy facades of bistros,
cafes and shops, where flush
tourists revel in luxury and glut,

while bundled millions
flow in wind-fed cold:
the workers and idlers,
driven by will or whim
over ice-slick sidewalks,
treading past townhouse,
brownstone and high-rise,
as we trail in thick coats
and boots, stepping fast
through red-brick plazas,

where lunchtime crowds
rush in snow-speckled air
amid vendors and beggars,
each glance exchanged
with a passing face
lost in the flux at once,
as cabs race for fares
with sprints and swerves,
their meters clicking faster
than an eye can blink.

At midday, the sun tilts west
to the Hudson, its stark piers
where junkies and whores
ply the kinks of their trades,
the swift tidal river a link
to the deep ocean lanes,
where cruise liners sail
like blood through veins
to far parts of the body,
pumped by the city's heart.

We stare at southbound ships,
the need to warm our bones
with a trip to tropic shores
unmet in our manic quest
for the next hip thing
that hurls us from dull job
to a hot new club or film
in the chilly urban whirl,
our hope of escape blown
seaward in freedom's wake,

as we file with the masses
down tight subway stairs,
the glares of foreign eyes
palpable on the platform,
where dark throngs lunge
through grinding turnstiles,
determined looks unfazed
by the loud jostling run
to packed cars, their speech
strange to our native ears,

the alien tongues ringing
in the tunnel, like those
of immigrants long gone
who tiled the mosaics
on these station walls,
their cut hands jammed
in pockets at nightfall,
when they shambled back
to congested tenements
on the island's margins,

where new accents now toll
among the dispossessed,
the plaintive rhythms and
idioms from ravaged lands,
the wails of dusty villages,
echoing in voices ever rootless
and misconstrued by Anglos,
words borne from distant soil,
spoken longingly at all hours,
haunting the tribal enclaves.

We start to trudge uptown
on weary legs, the stupor
of late afternoon a haze
that blurs cars and vans
to vague shapes stalled
in the long shadows
on roads and driveways.
We stop for a moment
to chart the sun, itself
unseen and angled off

to a red setting, the last
light caught by trim jets
that cruise in silence
along blue paths of sky
high above the Hudson
toward windy runways
of airports to the east,
where constant flights
whisk lives and goods
through the winter dusk.

But here on this drab block,
we resume our walk north,
boot scuffs and short breaths
marking the way at twilight,
when the island yields
to darkness, and merchants
toss sacks of trash to the curb,
pull grates of storefronts shut,
and lock their metal doors
with the firm *click* of a key.

The unlit edges and nooks
of the riverfront now thrum
as garbage trucks rumble
over jagged cobblestones,
unsheltered men mumble
on benches, and sea gusts
hum through narrow alleys,
lifting bits of litter skyward
to fly with a sharp wind
in the muted din of evening,

while the dimmed city turns
inward, its somber streets
dotted with lampposts,
headlights and neon signs
that jewel the night,
the lit windows of offices
and apartments blinking off,
the rows of sooty buildings
stolid in gray silhouette
along miles of lined blacktop,

where silence quells sound
for a few restless hours
before sunrise, until
the clash of word and noise
that spurred our strenuous
trek up this storied rock,
jolts us from bed again
to the clamoring pavement
and relentless tempo
of Manhattan's winter dawn.

Anima

The one who waits is the woman in me,
standing with the sunlight on her shoulders,
lying sleepless among shadows of night,
sitting at all hours with folded hands.

She waits in silence for another's touch,
feeling its warm pressure over her skin
and its frigid absence deep in her bones,
keeping the long vigil without demands.

Immigrant in Steerage

Alone in my berth, through unending night,
with only this rusted hull between me
and the sea's surge, I have neither red skies
of dawn and dusk nor stitches of starlight
for bearings, just a dull pulse of engines
and the sounds of strangers who stumble lost
in long dank passageways beneath the waves.

In the palms of my rough fisherman's hands,
the lines of life and heart and mind, obscured
by cuts and calluses, offer no chart
for the voyage of this cavernous ship,
where I who once sang aloud through the streets
of my village above a sun-blessed shore,
now wail from an iron cell in the depths.

The Statue of Liberty

Lit from within, as if in a trance,
she walks erect on a small island,
holding the torch of an ancient dream
and a tablet inscribed with the date
a new world was born. She steps away
from the broken shackles at her feet,
her back forever turned on the land
she stands for, the flow of her long robes
at one with the restless sea, her eyes
staring past the expectant faces
of those who sail into New York bay—
her gaze fixed on a far horizon.

Northern Reverie

It is winter here and the emptiness
of seascape extends in all directions.
This is the season of solitary walks
across miles of ice-crusted shoreline,
when the sun burns with a muted fire
and time slows against a gunmetal sky,
when the gulls alone are full of vigor
and scavenge in long drifts of debris
spread by the frigid tides. It is now

that my weariness with cold weather
leads to dreams of Caribbean beaches
dotted with palms, shells and bright
umbrellas, where warm tropic waters
relax my knotted body, as I swim
with over-arm stroke and even kick
to strengthen my limbs for the trek
to spring, which lingers so far away
from the snow along this frozen coast.

A Cord of Wood

My father and I
sit by the hearth
in separate chairs,
watching the glow
from this last batch
of hickory logs,

our sightlines meeting
in the spark-filled air
where tortuous fire
leaps from the grate,
the writhing flames
reflected in our eyes.

Green Vistas

I walk the hard and darkened streets
of Manhattan as winter thaws,
where steel and concrete choke the earth,
where nature can't unfold or flow.

Gaudy neon and bits of glass
sparkling in asphalt swell the night
with portents of spring that lead me
to a park on the river's edge.

My left hand flies from its pocket
to test the air. The air says, *Write,*
until trees are flaming with leaves,
until waves are emerald fire.

Daffodils

The yellow flowers
still shine true,
and the green stems
descend straight
to the ornate rim
of a crystal vase,
but water's illusion
bends the rootless
cut ends that seem
to grasp for life
in their serene
vessel of glass,
set at eye level
on the narrow sill
of an oval window,
the facets glittering
in a brittle beam
of early April light.

One Among Many

When I'm discovered in some other life,
curled within the smile on Judy's lips,
held in the steady gaze of my father's
blue eyes, or gripped in the handshake
of a buddy, remember that the ways
of love, with their lingering reflections
in beauty, power and friendship, led me

to find a place in the lives of others,
to enter their looks and gestures and stay
as close as skin. And when time dissolves
even the smallest bits of this body,
perhaps some who still carry me within
will show with a grin, a nod or a wave
that I was more than my life span allowed.

Begonia

The plant had flourished in spring and summer,
and even in the cool weeks of autumn,
sending out shoot after shoot, leaf after leaf,
each leaf green with a reddish hue,
each flower bearing four white petals,
dusted with silver, and a vibrant yellow tuft.

But as the cold of winter encroached,
it withdrew into itself, the shoots hanging
limp and lifeless, the once-bright leaves
bereft of shine, the flowers wilted
and brown, the tufts dissolved to powder.

When the last few petals fell away,
a poem took root and persisted
through this dormancy and beyond,
even as the earth awakened again,
and the plant emerged from its stillness,
turning to the sun and to spring.

Dijon

Two days of rain were just ending
as I drove through this ancient town,
eager for the chic of Paris,
when I saw a pale cathedral,
the sculpted medieval facade
awash in glancing cataracts
that gave the stones a golden shine,
until bursting into sunspots—

and I remembered that poem
by D.H. Lawrence, on the girl
he saw bathing at her window,
dripping her shoulders with water
from a sponge, rivulets sluicing
and glowing to gold in the folds
of supple skin, each swaying breast
a yellow *Gloire de Dijon* rose.

The Reflecting Pool

An invisible insect breaks the sheen
of a tree-rimmed pool, as widening rings

move out from the center to awaken
the April images reflected there:

the yellow and green of leaves, the purple
and white of flowers, rippling in circles

through streaks of sun, undulating as one
across the water, from the single touch

of an insect, whose quiet influence
extends to every inch of wooded shore.

The Liquid Rose

The man who holds this glass of wine
once held the rose to savor its red,
and see the shapes that it assumed
from bud to blossom, and breathe
the fragrance from its many folds.

That flower now lives in the red
liquid flowing warm to my lips,
my face afloat in its dark mirror,
the bouquet wafting from the rim
in wave after heady wave

that opens me to the rose life,
as I drink the richness of its red,
taking deep within me its shapes
and fragrance, becoming at last
the consumed and consuming rose.

Maystars

So frail the flowers, but strong their grasp
of the earth. They seem to grow everywhere.
Watery embankments hold them in clusters,
as a clear night sky holds the constellations.
In deep woods, they shine in twos and threes,
as jewels shine in the hair of a dark beauty.
Beside massive trees and rock formations,
they retain their poise in the cold shadows,
as the small often do before great threats.

Each flower has seven branching leaves,
green and slender, beneath seven petals,
white and pointed, and from their center,
seven sepals, tipped with yellow, curve up
in a circle. Though its blossom spans less
than an inch, and its lifetime is measured
only in days, this star of early spring
spreads across fields, forests and slopes,
to shine above the budding landscape.

The Bond

Between the pages, there were months and years
and empty spaces that almost kept me
from reaching you. *From generation
to generation,* the Psalm says, little matters,
mountain and grass, large and small, and yet
despite the consuming work of our days,
you at your ledgers, I at my notebooks,
we held to a ritual that spanned
the rush of time: through *the hurrying years*
of thankless labor and constant worry,
our nights by the fire, sitting in silence,
made us the measure of each other's flame.

My pen begins to fill another page
with words to navigate the cold spaces
that separate us now. *From age to age,*
the Psalm says, little matters, prose and poem,
long and short, all die away in the air
as if they were only murmurs, and yet
here we are at the borderline, reaching
across to each other: *a dream at daybreak,*
father and son, you in a new June grave,
still shining in the face of your one child,
who sits with an open notebook at dawn,
our nighttime fires burning on the page.

The Widow

She could not pass beyond her own tears,
the liquid veil that enclosed her eyes.
She said she would always see him
lying there: pale, paralyzed and dying.

She could not recall the liveliness
of his eyes in those final days,
the watery blue still flowing to her
as it had for forty-two years.

She would always see him at the last
moment, when the stream of light
from his face failed to reach her—
this radiant bride of so long ago.

Sleep

When night surf subsides
and slides back to sea,
a calm lulls the shore,

as water left behind
gathers in shallow pools,
where shiners trapped within

drift wide-eyed, beyond
the pull of sun and moon,
in dark stillness.

Judy

Her head lies still
upon my chest,
the face framed
by short black hair,
brown eyes shut
in hooded lids
and long lashes,
her arms relaxed
around my neck,
one pale breast
pressed to my ribs.
As I move a bit,
her lower body
shifts in sleep,
a full hip rising
beside my thin one,
the lightly veined
and muscled legs
tapering down
along my own,
her narrow feet
entwined with mine.

Flight

From a plane above Manhattan,
I see white clouds as surf and dunes
on the unbuilt shoreline far to the east.

In this bright-billowed heaven,
I am blessed to sail once again
along the ocean coast I was born to.